COOKING UP PARENTING SUCCESS

A Systematic Recipe Guide for Parenting in Year One

DR. KENCHERA INGRAHAM

Copyright

Cooking Up Parenting Success

Copyright © 2024 Dr. Kenchera Ingraham

Author: Dr. Kenchera Ingraham

All rights reserved. No part of this book may be reproduced, stored in a retrieval system, or transmitted in any form or by any means, electronic, mechanical, photocopying, recording, or otherwise, without the prior written permission of the publisher, Dr. Kenchera Ingraham

Edmonton, AB. Canada

ISBN: 978-1-7382894-0-0 (Paperback).
ISBN: 978-1-7382894-1-7 (E-book).

Scripture quotations are taken from the Holy Bible, New International Version®, NIV®. Copyright © 1973, 1978, 1984, 2011 by Biblica, Inc.™

For information about special discounts for bulk purchases, please contact [Your Publisher's Contact Information].

First Edition: [June 2024]

Foreword

Picture the sheer surprise and elation of discovering you're expecting twins during an ultrasound – the immediate rush of thoughts about coordinating matching outfits, capturing endless precious moments with your little duo, and the sheer joy of expanding your family. But hold on a minute! What if, in that same moment, you already have a 10-month-old bundle of joy at home? Suddenly, the excitement gives way to a whirlwind of practical concerns – how will you juggle the attention, the finances, and the sheer logistics of wrangling three under the age of two?

Let's dive into the real-life whirlwind that was Kenchera's world not too long ago. If that weren't challenging enough, stepping into the unexpected role of sole parent at home ushered in a wave of daunting uncertainties and unprecedented challenges. Amidst the chaos, one thing remained crystal clear – those babies were counting on her, and their futures brimmed with endless possibilities.

In this heartwarming and enlightening book, Kenchera discusses the systems she devised, inspired by the Holy Spirit, when it felt like the weight of the world was resting squarely on her shoulders. Survival wasn't just an option; it became a non-negotiable mission. Through her journey, she unearthed the resilience, resourcefulness, and sheer determination that dwelled within her, proving that with a dash of humour, a sprinkle of creativity, and a whole lot of love, any challenge can be conquered.

So, grab a cup of coffee (or let's face it, maybe a double shot of espresso!), cozy up with this book, and let's learn how Kenchera was able to manage the enormous duties ahead of her!

Be inspired as Kenchera's story unfolds – because when life throws you curveballs, sometimes all you need is a bit of faith, a supportive village, and a whole lot of determination to turn things around. Here's to embarking on this joyful and insightful journey with Kenchera – happy reading, everyone!

Shuranda Hall

Dedication

I dedicated this book and my life to Jesus Christ. Without His love, grace, and mercy, I would not be alive to write the words to follow. Secondly, I dedicate this book to myself; truly, I can do all things through Christ, who strengthens me. Lastly, this book is dedicated to my children, my Jesus' given gifts: Bailey, Isaac and Isaiah. In countless ways, each of you saved my life; thank you! I hope the nations you build will be greater from generation to generation, and Mommy loves you. Thank you for stretching me so I might learn, unlearn, and relearn systems to be a better mommy every day.

Preface

Three under Two: How?

This book is written from a realistic and vulnerable standpoint. I'm not here to pretend I am this perfect mom who has perfect systems and I'm out here winning every mom's goals. If it were not for the empowerment of the Holy Spirit, it would be a straight loss, but with Jesus, we win!

Let me be clear, three under two wasn't the plan but when your life belongs to Jesus, you know that His plans for your life are for 'good and not for evil' *"For I know the plans I have for you," declares the Lord, "plans to prosper you and not to harm you, plans to give you hope and a future."* (Jeremiah 29:11 NIV). But even knowing this, there were many days when I could not see or feel this scripture as true. In 2021, the Lord blessed me with a beautiful gift in the form of a baby girl. I was overjoyed. I was so overjoyed that I became content with having just her at the time. But Jesus! When my Bumble B was 10 months old, I found out I was pregnant again. Not only was I pregnant, but I was also pregnant with twins! It's one thing to be surprised by a pregnancy, but being surprised by a twin pregnancy was unreal. To say the least, I was shocked yet grateful.

With a new job, I could not visualize how I was going to make it through another pregnancy with a toddler. Adding fuel to the fire, 8 weeks into this twin pregnancy, my marriage came crumbling down like the walls of Jericho. So, if you're following, I now had; a 10-month-old, a new job, still postpartum, now pregnant with twins, a broken heart and a failed marriage all unfolding within weeks of each other.

I had many questions for my ex-husband, myself, my spiritual parents and of course, the Holy Spirit. Seeing my way out of what felt like a mess was impossible. But truly, Jesus has turned my mess into a message, and my challenge into a championship and I am grateful and humbled. So there. That's a summary of how I became a mommy of 3 under two.

Why Systems?

Writing this book while caring for three young children under the age of two required many systems, one system that I used to write this book is the use of knowledge through a book written by Emmanuel Adewusi who is the lead Pastor at Cornerstone Christian Church of God titled, *"Interconnected Systems: A Wisdom Manual."* It is also by privilege that I attend this church and engage with sermons on interconnected systems. I have been defended by systems through these teachings on various platforms. I learned that my natural gift provided by Jesus is to answer the question of how best I can achieve a task or goal and how best I can maximize the division of labour. Throughout the book, interconnected systems, and the revelations from the Holy Spirit about systems and myself changed the way that I approached and understood my natural gifting. Apostle Emmanuel explains, *"Through the visionary lens of an Apostle, we see the strategic placement of people, processes, technology, and governance to achieve a vision"* It is with this understanding that I write and share the systems I employed during the first year of being a mother to twins and a 17-month-old.

Using recipes (because I love to cook and a recipe layout is generally easy to follow), the use of processes, technology, people, and governance helped me not just to survive, but thrive. I use these four categories to help explain my systems and better equip you to develop your own systems through whatever season of parenting you are in. I need to make it very clear that my ability to develop and strategically engage systems is a direct result of the love and kindness of Jesus Christ; and for that, I am forever grateful.

Introduction

Like recipes, this book is filled with quick step-by-step recipes to help you cook up parenting success. I want to encourage you to read each section and recipe card as a blueprint or as a starting point. Most people try out a recipe as suggested a few times, and once they get the hang of the recipe, they add or take away ingredients to their liking; I encourage you to do the same here. When I first felt led to write this book, I felt ill-equipped. I didn't feel like I was qualified or that I had anything to share. Having a set of twins when my daughter was 17 months old while recently separated from my husband felt like a punishment from God. I had many questions and seemingly not many answers. It was not until I cried out to God that He showed me that what He was allowing me to experience was birthing my stories. And It was that word that kept me sound and focused. One day, while executing my daily care for my children, the Lord stopped me in my tracks and asked me to look at all the systems I had in place. It was then I realized that He gifted me with the ability to design, plan, and execute systems for parenting success.

I intentionally do not use phrases such as "single parents," "mommy success," or 'Daddy success," because this book is to help all parents and guardians. I hope you use this book to help you create, plan, adjust, and implement some or all of the systems to help you thrive as a parent. Also, use what you have! In this book, you will find tips to help you stretch your resources by multiplying or using them in maximized ways.

Key Lessons

Lesson 1: Purpose

Systems are meant to make what you do effective and efficient. If your system is not making life a little bit easier or more systematic, perhaps it requires revisions.

Lesson 2: Revision

Somewhere along the line, I learned that the wrong expectation leads to disappointment. As such, I needed to enter the world of systems with the expectation that they often require revisions. Walking into the life of systems with this expectation helps me understand that just because a system needs a revision doesn't mean the system was not good or effective. You will know that your system is no longer useful when it is not working anymore. In that case, it is time to make some revisions.

Lesson 3: Settings (Time and place)

As a parent, you will learn that what works in the morning doesn't necessarily work in the evening or throughout the night. Therefore, ensuring that you have different systems for different times of the day and even physical settings is critical to effective system development and management.

Lesson 4: Emotions

During a teaching of a series at the time called "Ask Pastor E," I learned that *"feelings are to enjoy life, not to determine life."* This word certainly became flesh in my life as I realized that I had to employ my systems whether I felt like it or not. I'm not saying that it is wrong to have emotions because heaven knows I have many of them, many times a day! I'm saying when you don't feel like getting out of bed to add water to your formula mixer before the night begins, ignore those feelings; get up and do it. You'll be grateful at 3 a.m. that you did.

In the chapters to follow, I approach each system with a few assumptions:

- The system won't work for everyone, and that's okay.
- Everyone has a different support system, including human, physical, and financial resources.
- Successful parenting may be defined differently for everyone.

Chapter 1

Feeding Systems

I mentioned earlier that feeding and sleeping are two different experiences and systems that need to operate independently. However, this does not mean that they are not connected. For me, everything was connected to sleep during the first year of life. My twins went through 16 to 20 bottles a day, and between all three children, about 24 diapers in a day. Yes, I agree, that's a lot! So, you can imagine that a system was essential for me to not just survive but thrive. I'll take you through a 24-hour period in hopes that it will help you understand the systems of thriving in the first year of being the amazing parent that you are already.

Feeding Technique

A fed baby is a fed baby. Yes, ideally, we would all like to have our children fed with breast milk. However, this is not always our reality for so many reasons. Some of us choose to feed by breastfeeding, bottle-feeding, or a combo. Whatever method you choose, you should be mindful of the tools/systems you can use to ensure that your feeding system is successful. If you are breastfeeding, you should think about questions like: Will I pump for milk? Will I solely breastfeed? Will I solely pump? How will I breast pump? If you're bottle feeding, you might want to start by asking questions such as: what type of bottles will I use (glass/plastic/anti-colic/round/narrow)? What will it cost (have an idea and try to prepare)? How will I sterilize and clean bottles? Where and how will I store them? How many will I need, and what sizes of bottles and nipples throughout the first year?

At the birth of my twin boys, Isaac and Isaiah, I combo-fed with breast milk (pumped and direct) and bottle-fed with formula. Again, the why is unimportant, but I'm happy to share what worked for me. I learned quickly that my boys consumed more food than my daughter (which makes sense since it was two of them). I also realized that breastfeeding my daughter left me with some unaddressed anxious feelings. Even the thought of breastfeeding made me anxious. With all that I had going on, I could not take one more thing that would weigh on me mentally, but I tried.

I made sure that I researched any tool and system out there to make this experience more manageable.

Feeding Schedule and Routine

Initially, I had a limited number of bottles that were under 5 ounces, so those bottles were washed by hand. At that time, it felt manageable because I had the wonderful support of loving mothers, friends, and a community that quickly became like family. Each day began with freshly cleaned bottles, typically starting at 7 am with a diaper change. For me, sleep and feeding were intertwined; I always wanted to ensure that after feeding my boys or my daughter, they would be ready for sleep. I didn't want to interrupt their sleep by changing a wet diaper immediately after a feed. So, my second system was always to change their diapers before starting a feeding session.

The feeding system requires quite a bit of adaptation as your little one(s) grows. However, for every system, principles do not change.

Transitioning to Solids

Every child starts solids at different ages based on their individual needs. Some may begin at four months, while others might start between six to seven months. Regardless of the timeline you choose, it's important to always prioritize meeting your child's unique needs and not compare your journey to that of other parents or children. Here are some tips I recommend: leverage technology to your advantage. There are many all-in-one machines available that can steam, process, or blend foods into various textures needed during the first year of life. Additionally, consider organizing your storage space efficiently. For instance, if your child is five months old and eating softer purees, using an ice tray to portion and freeze the food into labelled servings can save you time and effort. Having the right utensils and feeding stations is crucial. Invest in tools that help your child sit comfortably during meals, like a sit-me-up chair or a highchair as they grow older. Personally, I used a sit-me-up station in our playroom for smaller feeds and a highchair in the dining room for more formal meals like breakfast and dinner. These simple systems can make the transition to solids smoother for you and your little ones.

Feeding System Recipe Card

INGREDIENTS

- Age: 0-12 Months
- Bottles and nipples (size to age and digestion appropriateness)
- Formula making machines Electric bottle/milk warmers Cleaning agent for bottles/pump machines Available milk source (Breast milk/formula) Breastmilk storage bags

METHOD & TIPS

- Always try to have a surplus of your milk supply
- Always have designated storage areas and places for your milk
- Have feeding stations set up in every room that you frequent with 3 to 5 bottles
- Have a source of milk and water for feeding in those rooms
- Use your dishwasher to wash multiple bottles (with natural soap pods)
- Prep bottles in advance by scooping the formula into bottles before mixing them

Chapter 2

Sleep Systems

I know that sleep can be a controversial topic for many parents. I respect whatever approach you choose and what works best for your family. I'm not here to judge that; rather, I'm here to share what worked for me.

Sleep has its ebbs and flows. As a new mom to Bumble B, I had no idea what journey was before me; sleep continues to be a journey. I had no idea what sleep training was, what it meant, if I wanted to or needed to do it; I knew nothing! Bumble B was 7 months old, and I was completely exhausted and over the co-sleeping blessings and struggles. So, I opted to sleep train Bumble B. It was like life gave me and her a gift. She and I slept longer, better, and woke happier! The method I chose is not important here; what is, in my opinion, is that I chose to sleep train. I am not saying that sleep training is the be-all and end-all. However, I am saying that you need to identify a system early for sleep.

While I waited until Bumble B was 7 months old to sleep train (mainly because I was winging it and didn't know what I was doing) with my twin boys, Isaac and Isaiah, I was much more intentional. I knew that surviving three under two meant early sleep systems for me, so sleep training began from the first day of the twin's birth. "What does that mean?" you might ask. It meant giving the boys an opportunity to self-soothe. I must say that self-soothing for them looks a lot different because they were primarily bottle-fed and used pacifiers, whereas Bumble B was primarily breast-fed and did not use a pacifier. I was never one who liked the idea of pacifiers. However, I quickly adjusted and shifted my mindset when I realized the pacifiers were helping me. Unfortunately, my boys both suffered from acid reflux and colic. A combination of these two health challenges early in life created new complexities and new understandings in my mothering. I had to learn how to manage two children who are dependent on their pacifiers to soothe them, but that's the blessing of systems. They required constant learning of behaviours, patents, preferences, successes, and failures to ensure what you're doing is working for you. Please ensure that any sleep system you put in place works for you.

Sleep Training

From day one, I made a conscious effort to swaddle my boys, teaching them to find comfort in something other than just being cradled in my arms. Of course, I'm not suggesting not to hold your children; cuddle them because they need it, and so do you! What I learned was the importance of being mindful about how long, when, and how often we hold them to prevent a dependency on being held to soothe them to sleep. There are undoubtedly moments when snuggling your babies is necessary. I often found myself needing that physical closeness with my babies to remind me of three things: I am loved, I am lovable, and I am loving. Don't deny yourself or your children these precious moments. At the same time, don't deny your children the chance to learn to sleep independently.

Sleep training, in essence, is about allowing your children to drift off to sleep on their own. It doesn't take away from meeting their needs. If they're hungry during the night, feed them; if they need a diaper change, attend to it; if they seek comfort, offer it. However, once their needs are met, encourage them to fall asleep independently. I remember vividly my concern when I returned to work when Bailey was nine months old. She still relied on nursing and being snuggled for almost an hour before she would sleep independently. It made me realize that she hadn't been sleep-trained, and I had unintentionally hindered her ability to feel secure in different environments and to rest well.

This realization transformed my perspective on sleep training. It wasn't about depriving my children but empowering them and myself. Admittedly, the thought of sleep training with twins was daunting initially. However, I came to understand that the systems I had in place from their birth, guided by intuition and the support of the Holy Spirit, were gently leading them towards independent sleep habits all along.

Sleep Training & Feeding

Additionally, when it comes to sleep training or sleep routines in general, it's important to be aware of how babies can quickly associate sleep with feeding, leading to dependency. It's beneficial to avoid associating feeding directly with falling asleep. While feeding may naturally make them drowsy and ready for sleep, if possible, try not to let your children fall asleep during or immediately after eating. However, I understand firsthand how challenging this can be, especially when feeding occurs close to their scheduled sleep time. Balancing these aspects requires patience and adaptability, knowing that each child's needs and rhythms can vary.

Sleep Schedule Times

Speaking of schedules, routines are crucial for effective sleep systems, as I was reminded many times before my boys were born. It seemed daunting to establish a routine for newborns, especially twins, right from birth. However, with the guidance of the Holy Spirit and determination, we managed it from day one. My boys learned to wake together, sleep together, eat together, and, yes, cry together (though laughter came later!). Initially, it was quite challenging to synchronize their schedules. I had to wake one if the other woke up and vice versa, ensuring they ate, slept, and had diaper changes together. After a few weeks of this routine, they naturally fell into a rhythm of waking, sleeping, eating, and changing together.

Having them on this synchronized system was crucial for me. It gave me predictable times when everyone would be asleep or awake, allowing me to manage daily activities, take care of the house, and prepare for the next cycle. Admittedly, this approach to sleep systems may seem counterintuitive—who wants to wake a sleeping child? But in the end, it made life easier and more predictable amidst the chaos of having three little ones.

By four months old, my boys had naturally adjusted to this routine. They would fall asleep within seconds (most times) by 7 p.m. and wake up together around 7:15-7:30 every morning.

Start early, establish a routine, and be consistent with it. Understand your own goals for sleep, and if you choose to sleep train, ensure it aligns with your family's needs. Above all, always prioritize meeting your child's needs without neglecting your own.

Sleep Systems Recipe Card

INGREDIENTS

- Age: 0-12 Months
- Sleep sacs
- Infant swaddles
- Safe sleep space (mini cribs, cots, bassinet)
- Noise machine (Optional)
- Sheet (2 or more)
- Sleepers

METHOD

Step 1: Diaper change once they are awake and as needed

Step 2: Feed (bottle or breastfeed)

Step 3: Burp Well. Cuddle a little

Step 4: Once you see cues for sleep (See Tips below), put your little one down and let them learn to put themselves to sleep

Sleep Systems Recipe Card Con'td

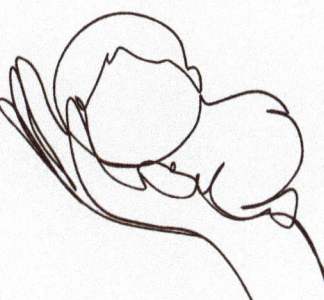

TIPS

- During the first 0-6 weeks, swaddle and allow babies to learn to sleep in a bright space and then transition to a dark space. This helps babies make the connection between night and day sleep
- Avoid rocking your baby to sleep; it becomes a dependency.
- Be consistent (e.g. diaper, feed, burp, nap)
- Have a designated space
- Sleeping babies in light during the first 6 weeks helps babies learn sleep cycles and the difference between day and night after that darkens the space
- Darken sleep space after 6 weeks (try blackout curtains or blinds)
- Make noise in those first 2-3 weeks
- Know your wake windows (see below)
- Use technology (e.g trackers, pen, paper)
- Communicate (Tell people)

Sleep Systems Recipe Card Con'td

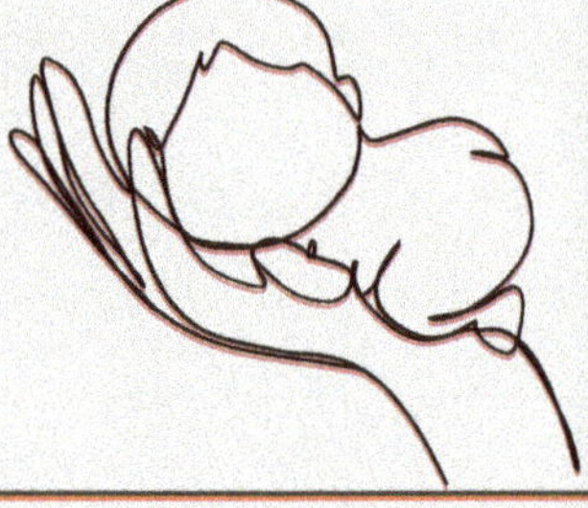

TIPS

- Don't compare (Parent the child you have and their needs)
- Schedule car rides around nap times (For example, I would schedule my daughter's daycare to drop off at the same time when the twins would be due for their first 30-minute nap of the day. If you nap first, then complete an errand, and they fall asleep on the car ride again, your sleep schedule is thrown off for the rest of the day.

Sleep Systems Recipe Card Con'td

TIPS FOR MULTIPLES

- Let them cry in the same room from birth. It becomes their personalized sound machine, and later on, they won't wake each other!
- If one baby wakes, wake the other (I know never wake a sleeping baby! But this does not apply to multiples if you want them in sync) When they wake together, they go back to sleep together.
- The morning wake is the most critical. Wake them at the same time, and the rest of the day will be "easy."

Sleep Cues:

- Especially for young babies, look for reddening eyebrows
- Yawning and rubbing eyes
- Rubbing your forehead into your chest
- One of my boys pulled his hair (your baby will tell you they need a nap)
- Becoming very quiet and not interested in play

Chapter 3

Toileting/ Diaper Changing Systems

When I think about toileting and diapering for children 0 to 1, I just think it is something that comes with the package. Many parents can foresee or think about the expense that often comes with dealing with this area of raising a child. One of the things I would suggest is finding a system and sticking to it until it is no longer working. If you're going to choose to go with cloth diapers, then create a budget, stick to it, and remember to pivot and adapt the system when it is no longer making life easier. If you're going with disposable diapers, then find the diaper that works for you. But not just the diaper that works for you but also your child and your budget. I'm not going to give you a prescriptive way to care for your child in this particular section, but rather just give you helpful tips on what worked for me. Again, this is just an approach. You can choose to modify it, take what you need, or leave it. Again, systems are not there to be prescriptive or rigid. They're there for you, to get you through a time and a season, and you must change and adapt your systems as you grow, as your children grow, and as you realize that this part of the system is not necessarily working for me at this time.

Diaper Schedule & Routine

A diaper schedule and routine require consistency, benefiting both you and your children. Kids quickly learn to anticipate diaper changes when they're part of a routine. However, having a routine doesn't mean strict times of day or ignoring your child's toileting needs if they're off schedule. In the early months, like the first week to two and a half months, one routine I established with my twin boys was changing their diapers immediately after they woke from a nap, which was every 2.5 hours at that time. I prepped a diaper with a wipe split in half, using ointment creams like petroleum jelly or diaper cream, and had everything ready when they woke. This routine continued with a bottle, a burp, and then back to nap time.

As your children grow, the sequence may change slightly, but having a diaper change right after waking ensures they're ready for the next nap without delays. Consider setting up diaper change stations around the house with essentials like spare clothes, wipes, diapers, bibs, and burp cloths. Having these stations handy reduces running around during stressful moments and makes it easier for helpers to assist in following your established routines. Sharing your systems with others may take some time initially, but it can prevent frustrations in the long run.

Managing Waste/ Diaper Output

When dealing with diaper waste, it's crucial to consider where that waste goes after your child soils their diaper. Odour control becomes a concern, especially with multiple children. Each parent has their preferred method, so it's about finding what works best for you. For me, I strategically placed Diaper Genies in various locations throughout my home, balancing accessibility and discretion. I also thought about the economics of diaper disposal, considering alternatives to traditional diaper bags. Searching for hacks from other parents can be helpful in this regard. To manage odour, I used car air fresheners and laundry scent beads in the diaper disposal units, along with baking soda, for its Odour-absorbing properties.

Ultimately, the key is to find a system that works for you and to adapt it as needed. Consider factors like the frequency of bag changes, disposal options outside of the Genies, and coordination with garbage collection schedules. Remember, dealing with diaper waste is a temporary phase, and with the right approach, you'll navigate through it smoothly.

Toileting / Diaper Change Systems - Recipe Card

INGREDIENTS

- Age: 0-12 Months
- Cloth or disposable diapers
- Single-use wipes of your choice / Washcloth or water
- Ointments
- Diaper genie/disposable bins
- Odour control: Baking soda, air fresheners, laundry scent balls, or car freshener clips.

METHOD

Step 1: Have diapers ready.

Step 2: Have cream and wipes ready.

Step 3: Check diapers and change before a nap.

Step 4: Once the child wakes up, change their diapers before feeding.

Step 5: Once you see cues for sleep (See Tips below), put your little one down and let them learn to put themselves to sleep.

Toileting/Diaper Change Systems - Recipe Card Cont'd

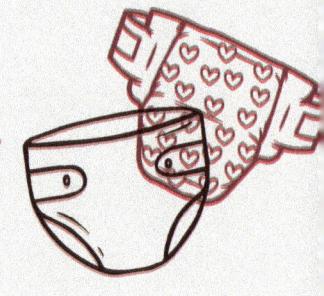

TIPS

- Have a schedule on how often you change your bins
- Check and dispose of your bins once everyone is asleep
- You can use a regular receptacle for pee diapers and change them daily
- A designated space
- Keep an eye out for sales and promotions on diapers and wipes
- Always set a budget and stick to it
- Don't stock up on smaller diapers because your child will grow out of them
- Stock up on larger diapers because your child will grow into them quickly
- If the diapers are disposable, they come with a landmark area at the front of the diapers, which indicates where the diaper fastens should fit for a perfect fit. If your child's diapers are not landing in that sweet spot of that mark out for fastening, then you might find that the diaper might be too small or too big

Chapter 4

Bath Time Systems

Bath time, often just before bed, is a key moment for parents to prepare for the bedtime routine. However, managing bath time can be challenging, especially with multiple young children. I integrated bath time into our bedtime routine, although it required careful coordination due to having two infants and a toddler. Every family approaches bath time differently, adapting to their unique circumstances and needs.

Bathing for me required continual adaptations. Where I was going to bathe them, how I was going to bathe them, the time of the evening I was going to bathe them, whether I was going to bathe all of them at the same time or bathe them individually. When my twins were born, one of the things I thought about was whether I bathed them before my 2-year-old got home from daycare or bathed her when I took a bath. So, early approaches for bathing required me to have a system, not just of what to do, but when I was going to do it; essentially, that time of the day.

One of the things I want to encourage parents to think about with bathing is to do the best you can with what you have and when you have it. I tried my best to always bathe my children every evening, but there were some days when it just was not feasible. Whether it was because they were unwell or not causing further delay to bedtime was more important, some days, a good wipe-down from head to toe was good enough. And with time I learned that this was okay.

I also did my best to think about my capacity. There were days where I was going on 2-3 hours of sleep so giving a bath wasn't something that I had the capacity to do, particularly on days like many of the days I had when I was alone. I didn't have the extra hand. I didn't have the extra help. And so, while I might have had the goal to bath my children every day, there were times when I just had to say out loud, "Kenchera, give yourself some grace. You're doing the best you can!" And that's the advice I want to give you as a parent. Give yourself some grace. You're doing the best that you can. Also, consider the setup of your home. Not every home has a bathtub. Not every home has multiple bathrooms. Not every home has multiple spaces or the actual physical space where you can change and adapt where you give baths. So, think about your life. Don't compare your parenting and bath time with how other parents do it or how they don't do it. Do the best you can with what you have and when you have the ability to do it.

Bath Time Systems Recipe Card

INGREDIENTS

- Age: 0-12 Months
- Skin-safe body wash
- Safe bath space (baby tubs/bath loungers)
- Bath towels
- (2) washcloths (One for body and one for mouth cleaning)
- Body moisturizer
- Change of clothes
- Change of Diapers
- Swaddle cloth
- Sleepers

METHOD

Step 1: Set everything up (bath water, toys, wash, after- bath body care and clothes)

Step 2: Run the water and check the temperature; run the water and use the back of your forearm to check the temperature. The temperature should be mild but warm enough to keep the body temperature of your babies.

Step 3: Give bath (Use this time to sing and talk and read books to your babies)

Step 4: Wash hair, behind the ears, crevices between the groin, elbow joints, under the arm, and the neck.

Bath Time Systems Recipe Card Cont'd

METHOD

Step 5: Introduce teeth brushing (Use a washcloth instead of a toothbrush)

Step 6: Dry well (Every crevice you washed is the crevice you dry to prevent rashes) special attention to the armpit, neck, behind the knee and ears)

Step 7: Moisturize and massage to help relax the baby

Step 8: Put on a fresh diaper (You can use an ointment of your choice to prevent diaper rash).

Step 9: Put on clean fresh clothes (Appropriate for size and temperature)

Step 10: Have a bottle ready and easily accessible.

Bath Time Systems Recipe Card Cont'd

TIPS

- During the first 0-6 weeks, use infant inserts. Consider swaddling the baby before and during baths to control body temperature and keep baths short.
- Be consistent (e.g., bath before bed and evening feed).
- A designated space (opt I always set up towels and clothes just outside the bathroom door on the floor).
- This time of the day can be overwhelming (keep encouraging yourself; a lot is happening quickly, but it's almost bedtime!).

TIPS FOR MULTIPLES

- Bath them together
- Baths don't have to happen in the bathroom. Sometimes, I would set up in my bonus room so I could keep an eye on my 2-year-old. Just use towels or shower curtains under the bathtub to keep the floor dry. Have an assembly line set up with clothes, towels, creams, etc, on each bath towel.

Chapter 5

Caring for your home

Managing household chores and caring for your home can be a significant challenge, especially as children grow and become more active. I think about all the areas that need attention—kitchen cleaning, maintaining living spaces, bathrooms, children's bedrooms, laundry, and more. It's essential to find ways to manage these tasks while also prioritizing personal well-being and spiritual health. Having a system in place is crucial. This might involve seeking help from neighbours, friends, and family, or using technology like robot vacuums. Setting rules and expectations for cleanliness within the house is also helpful, such as teaching children to clean up after themselves. For example, my daughter has a system where she organizes her toys into zip-lock bags after playing. This keeps her play area tidy and makes it easier for her to find what she wants next time.

In terms of laundry and dishwashing, finding efficient methods is key. I realized I could simplify laundry by using gentle laundry soap for everyone's clothes instead of separating them. This reduces the hassle of sorting laundry and keeps things more organized. I also hired help to assist with tasks like folding laundry, making the process smoother and less overwhelming for me. These strategies, along with others like using the dishwasher efficiently and keeping the bathroom clean, contribute to a more manageable and enjoyable home environment. In the next pages, we'll delve into specific systems and tips for maintaining a clean and organized home.

Caring for Your Home - Recipe Card

Recipe Card for Laundry

INGREDIENTS

- Laundry Soap
- Washing machine & Dryer
- Baskets
- People
- Time
- Capacity
- Distilled vinegar
- Baking soda

METHOD

Step 1: Drop items as you use them into the washer S

Step 2: Sort three loads to go into the dryer

Step 3: Load in the dryer (whites, colors, towels/sheets)

Step 4: Place in laundry baskets

Step 5: Enlist people or yourself to fold, organize, and put away

Caring for Your Home - Recipe Card Cont'd

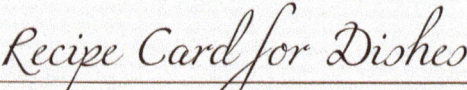

Recipe Card for Dishes

INGREDIENTS

- Dishwasher
- Dishwashing liquid/detergent.

METHOD

Step 1: Load the dishwasher to maximum potential and leave the top rack for bottles.

Step 2: Arrange bottles with their covers in the center of the top rack.

Step 3: Line the sides of the top rack with both short and tall bottles.

Step 4: On the other side of the top rack, place glasses, mugs, and glassware, optimizing the space used.

Caring for Your Home - Recipe Card Cont'd

Recipe Card for Babysafe Spaces

INGREDIENTS

- Baby proof equipment
- Favourite cleaning products

METHOD

- Baby-proof areas to prevent clutter and dirt and continuous cleaning of areas of the entire house and it confines everything to a central space that you can mentally, emotionally and physically manage to see less clean but manageable to clean when possible.

Caring for Your Home - Recipe Card Cont'd

Recipe Card - Cleaning Systems

INGREDIENTS

- Favourite cleaning products (I use vinegar with some essential oil, natural soap, and food-grade peroxide)
- Vacuums
- Dusters
- Organizing Bins
- Headphones and an Audiobook

TIPS

- You can hire a babysitter for two hours so you can focus on cleaning or when they are taking a nap.
- The use of vinegar and baking soda on all clothes; neutralizes odour, softens clothes and removes stains naturally and effectively!

METHOD

Step 1: Start at the end of the day when kids are in bed

Step 2: Find one area of the house to tackle for the evening

Step 3: Find one area and load the dishwasher

Step 4: Prepare for the next morning; replenish items used the day of (diaper bins, water, and formula in machines, clean bottles)

Step 5: Set a day that you would routinely clean bathrooms and tidy around the house.

Caring for Your Home – Recipe Card Cont'd

External Home Care – Recipe Card

INGREDIENTS

- Lawnmower
- Snow Shovel
- Snowblower
- Time

TIPS

- Do this when you have the time and capacity to do it
- Hire someone to do it when you are not able to do it yourself
- Ask for help, including your neighbours

Chapter 6

Caring for Yourself

When I talk about caring for yourself, this is often a subject I have with mothers who feel they don't have enough time. I repeatedly talk to Moms about it. I get it. I know what it feels like not to have enough time to take care of yourself. It feels like you don't have time to wash your hair, get a massage, or take care of your physical, emotional, and spiritual health. It seems like there's so much going on, and everything seems to be a priority. But guess what? You can only care for others as much as you care for yourself. You have to be able to pour from a glass that has something in it. You can't pour from an empty cup. So this might seem like the most challenging chapter to comprehend or wrap your mind around, but the truth is you can do it. Once you're intentional about doing it, you can choose you. And I want to congratulate you right now on choosing you because you're worth it. You spent time and energy bringing your kids into the world, so you must think about how to sustain yourself. When I say think about yourself, I mean to think of yourself as a whole. Another thing I did was commit myself to going on retreats. There is an organization called *Women's Intermission* that was created to intentionally give women an opportunity for an all-inclusive weekend getaway to *"Rest. Regroup. Rest. And Recharge."* I schedule this in my year and start asking for babysitting coverage months in advance. It makes all the difference in having something to look forward to and a chance to Rest. Regroup. Rest. And Recharge.

My spiritual life is the most important to me. It helps me have the wisdom and revelation to balance caring for three children with my mental and physical work. Caring for yourself is one of the areas that I think parents often neglect because you're supposed to have it together. For me, my mental health was a great challenge in this season. It was something I had to be intentional about. At the time, I was going through a separation. I experienced a devastating hurt in my marriage when I found out I was eight weeks pregnant with my twins. My daughter was just 13 months old. My mental health began to deteriorate. I began to struggle with suicidal thoughts, anger, resentment, and hatred. This continued even up to three to four months after pregnancy.

I had to catch myself; otherwise, my children would have been orphans. The thought of my children being orphans shook me to my core and made me think about intentionally working on my mental health. I couldn't save my mental health myself, but I knew I had a saviour, Jesus. During that season, I still loved Jesus. I knew He was real, and everything He did was intentional.

I also had to recognize that this situation was a season and not a lifetime. I had questions: What did I want my life to look like when this season changed? Do I want to be in a position where I no longer recognize myself? Would I be able to look at my scars and say that what came to break me did not break me, and instead, it built me? I hope that as a parent, you will not see your tough season as a time to break you but a time to build you.

When considering self-care, it's vital to view yourself holistically. It's not just about physical health or hitting the gym; it's about nurturing your spiritual, mental, and emotional well-being too. These aspects are interconnected and play a significant role in how we parent and nurture our children.

Building a strong spiritual foundation can provide guidance and strength during challenging times. For me, discovering Christian meditation was transformative. It allowed me to connect with God's word deeply, leading to spiritual growth and insight. I found that this spiritual nourishment positively impacted my physical health as well. I became more mindful of what I ate and drank. I even incorporated physical activities like using my babies as weights during exercises, which brought joy and vitality to my routine.

Moreover, focusing on positive thoughts and truths, especially in moments of stress or worry, can shift our mindset and bring about a sense of peace and empowerment. By meditating on God's promises and embracing positive affirmations, I began to speak life into myself and my role as a parent. I recognized that I am whole, capable, and blessed, and I passed on this positivity to my children, creating a nurturing and loving environment for them to thrive. I encourage you to research and subscribe to *"Hour of Meditation" on* YouTube by Dr. Emmanuel Adewusi.

So, as you navigate your journey of self-care, remember to consider your whole self. Embrace practices that uplift your spirit, sharpen your mind, and nourish your emotions. Whether it's through meditation, prayer, positive affirmations, or other holistic approaches, prioritize your well-being. You deserve it, and your children will benefit from a parent who is balanced, resilient, and full of love. Keep caring for yourself, and may God bless you abundantly.

Caring for Yourself Recipe Card

INGREDIENTS

- Decisions: Thinking outside of the box
- Capacity
- Financial Resources
- Social Platforms
- Eating well
- Meditation
- Prayer
- Study of the Word and reading books
- Community; People
- Time and grace

TIPS

- Use the stairs in your house for physical exercise
- Be intentional and make it a part of your everyday activity.
- Use opportunities to take care of your home as a chance to take care of yourself
- You don't 'need' a separate time to read or spend time with God. You can do these things as you're working, cleaning, and taking care of your home.
- Hire or ask for help when you need it

Caring for Yourself Recipe Card Cont'd

TIPS

- Give yourself 4 to 6 hours alone every 3 or 4 weeks
- Read audiobooks while you clean
- Use free exercise programs where available, like YouTube or other social platforms.
- Go for walks, and you can take your baby; organize your nap time so you can kill two birds with one stone.
- Train yourself to think positive thoughts every time negative thoughts come to mind
- Meditation: Meditation helps us build not only our spirits but also our minds
- Spiritual: Find a good home-based Bible-based church and build a community with like-minded people.

A Prayer of Salvation

Dear Lord Jesus,

I come to you today. I believe you are the Son of God and that you died for my sins and resurrected on the third day to give me life. Today, right now, I accept you into my heart and I put my faith in you.

CONGRATULATIONS
WELCOME TO THE FAMILY OF GOD

If you said the prayer, and you don't have a Home church, please scan the QR code and we would be happy to connect with you.

If you do have a home church, please connect with your Pastor for further guidance.

www.ingramcontent.com/pod-product-compliance
Lightning Source LLC
Chambersburg PA
CBHW061742070526
44585CB00024B/2776